Hello，旧金山

[美] 刘威廉◎著　纪钧译◎绘

Hello, San Francisco

当代世界出版社
THE CONTEMPORARY WORLD PRESS

版权登记号：图字 01-2021-1938 号

图书在版编目（CIP）数据

Hello，旧金山：汉文、英文 /（美）刘威廉著；纪钧译绘，— — 北京：当代世界出版社，2021.7

ISBN 978-7-5090-1587-2

Ⅰ．①H… Ⅱ．①刘… ②纪… Ⅲ．①旅游指南 – 旧金山 – 儿童读物 – 汉、英 Ⅳ．① K971.29-49

中国版本图书馆 CIP 数据核字 (2021) 第 032515 号

书　　名：Hello，旧金山
出版发行：当代世界出版社
地　　址：北京市东城区地安门东大街 70－9 号
网　　址：http://www.worldpress.org.cn
责任编辑：李俊萍
编务电话：（010）83907528
发行电话：（010）83908410（传真）
　　　　　13601274970
　　　　　18611107149
　　　　　13521909533
经　　销：全国新华书店
印　　刷：北京博海升彩色印刷有限公司
开　　本：787 毫米 ×1092 毫米 1/12
印　　张：3.5
字　　数：20 千字
版　　次：2021 年 7 月第 1 版
印　　次：2021 年 7 月第 1 次
书　　号：ISBN 978-7-5090-1587-2
定　　价：49.00 元

特别感谢：

中文老师：我的姥爷和姥姥

Colleen Golden, Reading Specialist, English Language Support/ELPAC Assessor

Richard C. Alexander Bac

以及所有关爱和帮助我的家人们

文字作者简介

刘威廉，8岁，幼儿园时移居美国旧金山。到旧金山后，威廉开始学习不同的语言与文化，并在学习过程中享受到书写的快乐。他的英语水平提升很快，同时坚持学习中文，对中英文运用自如。他希望用中英双语的形式给大家分享旧金山的风貌，于是有了这本书。

William Liu, 8 years old, moved to San Francisco when he was in kindergarten. William began to learn different languages and cultures after moving to San Francisco, He enjoys the fun of writing during the learning. His English has been improved rapidly. In the mean while, he insists on learning Chinese. He hopes to share the city scape of San Francisco in both Chinese and English, That's why he has written this book.

绘画作者简介

纪钧译，画家，毕业于天津美术学院，曾在加拿大温哥华举办个人油画风景作品展“可见之诗”，并于2018年获得第十二届国际青少年艺术节“国际优秀导师奖”。

2019年其作品《婺源古村落》被编排进中国国家十三五规划教材《造型基础》；2020年其作品《海边的余晖》获得美国第十届海景在线大赛“特别表彰奖”。

Junyi ji, the painter, graduated from Tianjin Academy of Fine Arts. His personal landscape oil paintings exhibition “Visible Poetry” was held in Vancouver, Canada.He was also given “International Outstanding Mentor Award” at the 12th International Youth Art Festival in 2018.

An Ancient Village in Wuyuan, an oil painting, was compiled in *Basic Modelings*, one of the China’s 13th Five-Year Plan textbooks in 2019; He was given “Award of Special Recognition” for his painting *Afterglow by the Sea* in the 10th Online Seascape Competition of the United States in 2020.

绘画作品简介

该书中的作品是用平板手绘创作而成，传统的绘画技巧和现代科技相结合，绘画工具从颜料、毛笔转化为电子笔，使画面新颖而有趣。绘画的笔触单纯而有力量，简约而不简单，不同的景色用不同的色调来表现，使主题更加突出、色彩更加鲜明，让读者如身临其境。

The drawings in the book are hand-painted on the Ipad. Traditional painting skills combined with modern science and technology, and painting tools transformed from ink and brush to electronic pen, have made the drawings creative and interesting. The brushwork is simple and powerful, brief but not simple. Different landscapes are represented by different colors which highlight the theme and make the colors more brightful. They are so vivid that readers would feel as if they were right on the scene.

C目录NTENTS

01 旧金山所在地

中英对照，语音领读
手机扫一扫，立即领取

San Francisco is a city in Northern California.

it's by the Pacific Ocean. The water by the city is called the San Francisco Bay.

旧金山是美国加利福尼亚州北边的一座城市。

它坐落于太平洋沿岸，被太平洋环绕的地区，形成了旧金山湾。

WELCOME
TO
SAN FRANCISCO

02

旧金山的地貌

San Francisco is a hilly city with more than 50 hills.

People use cable cars to get up and down the hills. The cable cars run on tracks. They do not have an engine. They have electric motors.

旧金山是一座山地城市，有 50 多座山丘。

人们使用缆车出行。缆车在轨道上行驶，它们没有引擎，需要靠电来运行。

03
金门公园

A great place for kids to visit in San Francisco is Golden Gate Park.

The Park has a really cool science museum called the California Academy of Sciences with an aquarium.

对孩子来说，旧金山有一个极好的去处，那就是金门公园。

金门公园里有非常酷的加州科学博物馆，博物馆的里面有一个水族馆。

At the park you should also visit Stow Lake.

At Stow Lake, you can rent bikes that hold 6 people or rent a boat and go to the waterfall. Be sure to bring some crackers to feed the ducks and swans.

Last, go to the best Children's Playground.

It has a super-fast cement slide, carousel and delicious snacks. Golden Gate Park is awesome for kids.

金门公园里的斯托湖也非常值得一看。

在湖边，你可以租一辆可供六人骑行的自行车或租一艘船前往瀑布。记得带一些饼干去喂鸭子和天鹅。

最后，一定要去儿童游乐场，那可是最好的儿童游乐场。

那儿有滑起来速度超快的水泥滑梯、旋转木马以及美味的小吃。金门公园真是很棒的地方。

04
金门桥

One of the most famous bridges in the world is in San Francisco, the Golden Gate Bridge. It is 8,981 feet long. It is a suspension bridge over the San Francisco Bay.

The Golden Gate Bridge is a red-orange color. This color was chosen so it is visible in the San Francisco's fog. The city is often foggy and windy, so it's a good idea to dress in layers.

跨越旧金山湾的吊桥叫金门桥。

它是世界上最著名的桥梁之一，长 8,981 英尺。金门大桥的颜色是橙红色的。之所以选择橙红色是因为旧金山经常有雾且多风，这样它就能在雾中仍然被看见。给金门大桥穿上这件橙红色的外衣真是个好主意。

05
珍宝蟹

California Dungeness Red Crab is the most famous seafood in California.

You can easily catch that crab in California.

It goes best with butter. The best way to serve it is fresh out of sea boiling, that way it is much fresher.

珍宝蟹是加州最有名的美食。

你在加州很容易钓到这种螃蟹，涂上黄油的珍宝蟹吃起来味道好极了。

从海里捞上来后直接用水煮是最好的做法，这样做真是无比鲜美。

06
酸面包

Sourdough bread is famous in San Francisco. Boudin bakery located in Fisherman's Wharf has been baking bread for 171 years.

The Boudin sourdough bread has only four simple ingredients: flour, water, salt and a piece of sourdough.The inside of the sourdough tastes soft and fluffy, like biting into a piece of a cloud. While the outside crust

Hello. 旧金山

酸面包是旧金山最有特色的美食。Boudin 面包店位于渔民码头，已经有171年的历史。制作酸面包只需要四种简单的食材：面粉、水、盐和酸面团。酸面包的里层吃起来松软可口，就像咬着一团云朵，而外皮却很松脆。旧金山的空气是最适合酸面包发酵的，所以，全世界最好吃的酸面包在旧金山。酸面包是非常健康的食品。

is very crunchy. The San Francisco weather helps to make the best sourdough bread. It is very healthy and good for people.

07
半月湾

Looking for a place to visit outside the city? Halfmoon Bay is a short car ride away. On the drive to Halfmoon Bay you can see beautiful views of the Pacific Ocean.

In Halfmoon Bay you can walk on the beach and visit tide pools where you will see fish and seaweed.

想去看看城外的风景吗?

从旧金山开车很快就可以抵达半月湾，路上还可以欣赏太平洋的美景。在半月湾的海滩上漫步，可以透过清澈的海水看到鱼和海藻。这里的饭店供应多种美味的海鲜。蝴蝶面包和饼干上的盐也是来自大海哦，在半月湾的海边可以看到很多海鸥，码头上的渔民在船上卖鱼，你可以买到整条的三文鱼。

The restaurants in Halfmoon Bay serve lots of delicious seafood. The bread and pretzels salts are even from the sea too! You can see lots of seagulls. The fisherman sell fish on their ships. You could buy a whole salmon.

08
九曲花街

Lombard Street is one of the world's steepest and curvest street. The road has lots of beautiful flowers.

You can drive down the street, but you need to be very good at driving.

九曲花街是我见过的最陡峭、最弯曲的街道。

街道两边有很多好看的花。

你可以开车穿过街道，前提是你的开车技术要很好。

09 动物园

The San Francisco Zoo is located between Lake Merced and Pacific Ocean. The San Francisco Zoo has lots of interesting things to explore.

You can see different types of animals like amphibians, mammals, reptiles, invertebrates, birds...

When you walk outside the zoo, you are only a 1-2-minute walk to the Pacific Ocean.

旧金山动物园在默塞德湖和太平洋之间。

动物园里有很多有趣的地方，你可以看到不同种类的动物：两栖动物、哺乳动物、爬行动物、无脊椎动物、鸟类等。

当你从动物园出来，往前走一两分钟，就可以走到太平洋岸边。

10
要塞公园

The Presidio of San Francisco has been around for over 200 years. It was originally a military base that was then transferred into a Public National Park in 1994.

One of the best things to do here is visit the Walt Disney Family Museum. You can see how Walt Disney made the cartoons.

要塞公园有 200 多年的历史。它原来是军事基地，后来在 1994 年被改建为国家公园。

这里最好玩的地方是华特·迪士尼家庭博物馆，你可以在这里看到华特·迪士尼是如何制作动画片的。

11
双子峰

Twin Peaks is a must to visit.

It has 360-degree view of the San Francisco Bay Area.

Twin Peaks has mountains about 900 feet.

You can see lots of the tourist attractions.

你一定要去双子峰，那里可以 360 度俯瞰旧金山湾区。

双子峰海拔约 900 英尺，因此你可以远远地看到很多旅游胜地。

12
39 号码头

Pier 39 is one of the world's most famous places to see sea lions.

There are wooden boards that the seals relax on. At Pier 39 there are many interesting shops and seafood restaurants.

39号码头是世界上著名的观看海狮的地方，这里有许多木板，海狮们常常慵懒地躺在上面享受阳光。39 号码头还有很多有趣的商店和海鲜餐厅。

PIER
39

13
海湾水族馆

Aquarium of the Bay has lots of local marine animals.

At the Aquarium there is a tunnel under the water, you can see sharks, bat rays and fish swimming all around you, even over your head.

海湾水族馆里有很多当地的海洋动物。

水族馆有一条水下隧道，在这里，你可以看到鲨鱼、蝙蝠鱼和其他鱼类环绕着你游来游去，有时甚至会在你的头顶嬉戏。

14
唐人街

San Francisco's Chinatown is the largest Chinatown outside of Asia. It is the oldest Chinatown in North America. Visitors should enter through the famous Dragon Gate. Chinatown has lots of shops with many cultural items similar to those of China. You can make your own fortune cookies and taste dim sum and other traditional Chinese foods. This is the place where you can buy lots of souvenirs. If you want to know modern China, you should visit China!

旧金山的唐人街是亚洲以外最大的唐人街，也是北美地区最早的唐人街。著名的龙门是唐人街的入口，这里有很多有中国文化特色的商店。你可以品尝到美味的点心和其他中国传统美食，还可以制作自己的幸运饼。这里是购买纪念品的好去处。不过，如果你想了解真正的中国，还是去中国看看吧！

天下為公